1ST CLARINET

OVERTURE

by Jim Engebretson, Quincy C. Hilliard, Jim M
Steve Toren, Mark Williams, Vic Williams, and

CONTENTS

INSTRUMENTATION

Conductor	Bass Clarinet	1st Trumpet	Baritone B.C.
Flute	Bassoon	2nd Trumpet	Baritone T.C.
Oboe	Alto Saxophone	F Horn	Tuba
1st Clarinet	Tenor Saxophone	E Flat Horn	Drums
2nd Clarinet	Baritone Saxophone	Trombone	Auxiliary Percussion
Alto Clarinet			

FOREWORD

Although designed for the *Ed Sueta Band Method*, OVERTURE can be utilized with any band method after the introduction of eighth notes.

IRONVIEW MARCH

1st B♭ CLARINET

JIM ENGEBRETSON

KUM BA YAH

1st B♭ CLARINET

Arr. by JIM MEREDITH

MOUNDSDALE CHA CHA

1st B♭ CLARINET

JIM ENGEBRETSON

CHORALE AND MARCH

1st B♭ CLARINET

VIC WILLIAMS

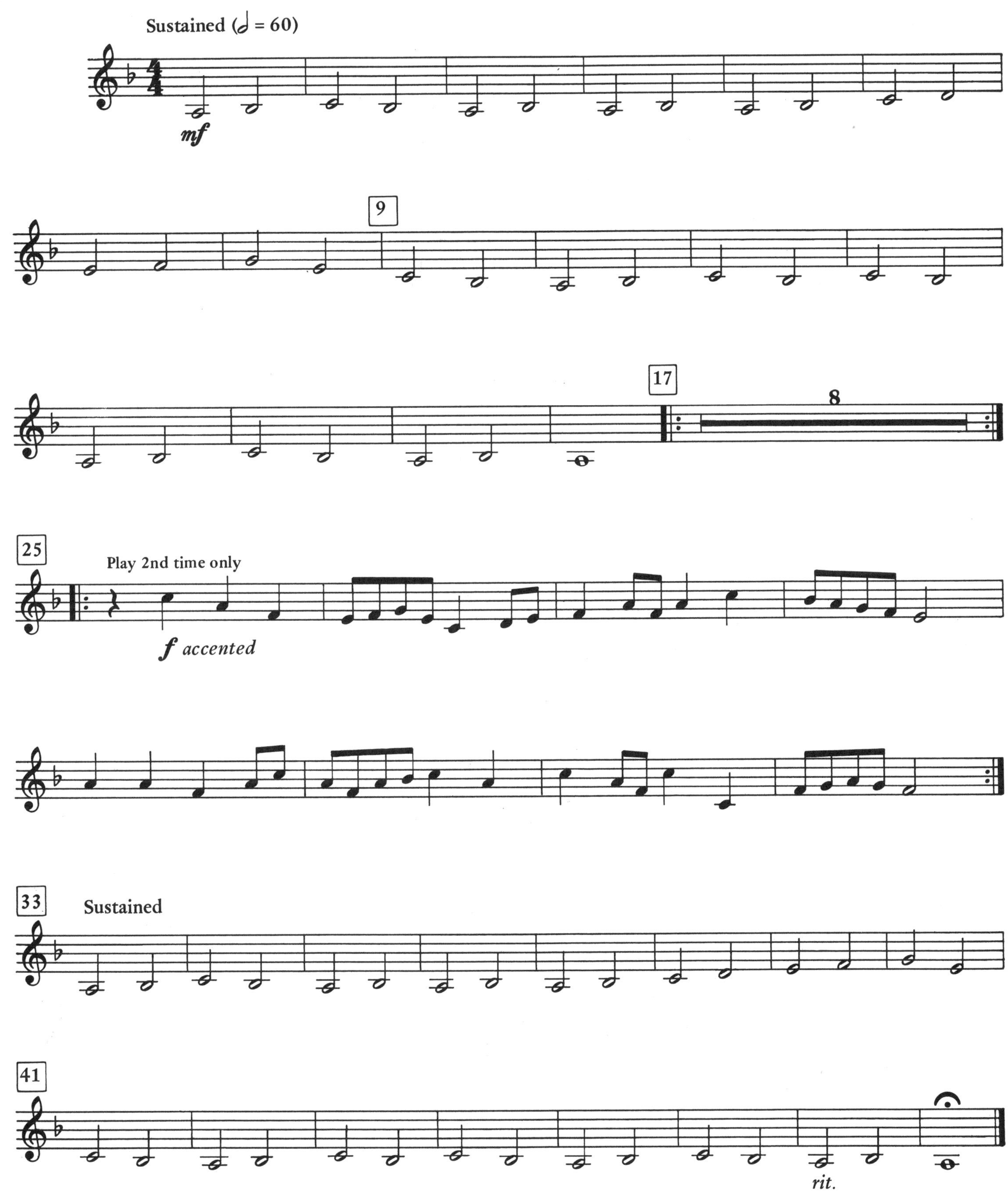

CHOO-CHOO BLUES

1st B♭ CLARINET

QUINCY C. HILLIARD

GROOVIN'

1st B♭ CLARINET

QUINCY C. HILLIARD

AMBLESIDE MARCH

1st B♭ CLARINET

STEPHEN TOREN

M.F.A. CHA CHA CHA

1st B♭ CLARINET

ED SUETA

CLOVERLEAF WALTZ

1st B♭ CLARINET

QUINCY C. HILLIARD

ROCKIN' EASY

1st B♭ CLARINET

ED SUETA

LITTLE CHIEF

1st B♭ CLARINET

QUINCY C. HILLIARD

THE SAINTS

1st B♭ CLARINET

Arranged by ED SUETA

ROYAL PROCESSIONAL

1st B♭ CLARINET

MARK H. WILLIAMS

HILL CITY RAG

1st B♭ CLARINET

JIM MEREDITH

Brightly (♩ = *ca.* 116-126)

PASEO DEL RIO

1st B♭ CLARINET

VIC WILLIAMS